Stress-free Wedding

Wishing you a blissful wedding planning journey –

With love,

Stress-free Wedding

Caroline Lacaille-Gaudy

Stress-free Wedding

The guide to planning your wedding with ease and calm.

And tools to use forever in your marriage and in all areas of your life.

Caroline Lacaille-Gaudy

Stress-free Wedding

Table of Contents

If You're The Type Who Only Reads One Chapter, This Is The One
11

What exactly is BLISS by Caroline?
17

Our atypical love story
23

SECTION 1 Stress Management

It's Not What You Think
33

Your Mind: The Wedding Crasher
37

Stress: The Uninvited Guest
43

Taming the Wedding Stress Monster
49

SECTION 2 Crafting Your Shared Vision

Your Brain is a Party Animal (With Some Questionable Guests)
63

Your Beliefs: The Secret Sauce (or Saboteur) of Your Relationship
71

Your Wedding, Your Way: Designing Your Dream Day
77

Sharing Your Vision
93

SECTION 3 Enjoyment Enhancers

Why Building A Dream Team Is Crucial
97

Selecting Your Dream Team
101

SECTION 4 Your Biggest Stressors

Yes, It's Finally Time To Talk About Your In-Laws (And Other Challenging Family Dynamics)
109

Navigating Conflicts
127

Let's Talk About Money
139

SECTION 5 Your Wedding Day

Enjoying Your Blissful Day
147

You Are The Star Of Your Day
151

SECTION 6 Your Journey Beyond Your Wedding Day

It Only Takes You
159

Afterword
165

The Author
167

Acknowledgments
171

Access The Bonuses
175

First published in 2024
© Copyright Caroline Lacaille-Gaudy
All rights reserved. No part of this publication may be reproduced, stored in or introduced into a retrieval system, or transmitted, in any form, or by any means (electronic, mechanical, photocopying, recording or otherwise) without the prior written permission of the author.

This book may not be lent, resold, hired out or otherwise disposed of by way of trade in any form of binding or cover other than that in which it is published without the prior written consent of the Author.

Whilst every effort has been made to ensure that information in this book is accurate, no liability can be accepted for any loss incurred in any way whatsoever by any person relying solely on the information contained herein.

No responsibility for loss occasioned to any person or corporate body acting or refraining to act as a result of reading material in this book can be accepted by the Author, or by the employers of the Author.

Contact the author:
Caroline Lacaille-Gaudy
blissbycaroline.com
book@blissbycaroline.com

Cover image © BLISS by Caroline & Caroline Lacaille-Gaudy
Illustrations by Caroline Lacaille-Gaudy unless otherwise mentioned.

I dedicate this book to the lovers who want to make their wedding planning and wedding day the beginning of the most amazing chapter of their life.

I hope that the ideas and tools in this book assist you in creating a celebration that reflects your unique love story.

***

To the two most important people in my life: JL & Louise.
Thank you for your unwavering support and unconditional love. Through highs and lows, there is no one else I'd want to do life with.

Stress-free Wedding

If You're The Type Who Only Reads One Chapter, This Is The One

I intentionally wrote a tiny book (because I know how busy you all are), filled with practical tools (so you can apply what you read). But if you still feel like it is too much, I've made the most concise summary here.

If you are planning on reading the whole book, feel free to skip this chapter for now and enjoy the read. I hope you find it helpful.

Here is a high-level summary of what is covered:

Stress Management (Chapter 1 & 3): The key insight is that what stresses you out is not the root cause and rather a symptom. Your parents, in-laws, the timeline, the decisions, the budget... None of these are stressful, but they might be to you because there is something much deeper going on for you. And if you decide to change your response to your stressors by simply becoming aware of the reasons why these things give you stress, half the battle will be won.

How Your Mind Works (Chapter 2): Most people believe that what they think is coming from them. Robin Sharma said "The mind is a wonderful servant but a terrible master." If you let your mind control your life you will end in discomfort and stagnation. It's only when you decide to reclaim your power over your mind and tell it what to think, that your life can transform. And believe me when I say 'it feels like magic' when you do.

Lower Your Stress Level (Chapter 4): Prioritizing your self-care is the biggest game-changer for your well-being and to lower your stress. If you do only one thing in this area: sleep. Good quality and enough sleep is deeply transformative. There are more ideas in the chapter including fun ones ;).

Level Up Your Beliefs (Chapter 5 & 6): What you believe creates your reality. Becoming aware of your most unconscious beliefs about marriage, love, and your wedding day can help you notice what is holding you back from having the wedding you truly desire. You get to choose what you believe, it's that simple (and yet not easy).

Craft A Powerful Vision (Chapter 7 & 8): Your wedding vision goes beyond a mood board and inspiration pins. If you do only one thing to minimize stress and get the wedding you want, design a vision so crisp (tapping into all senses and feelings), that everyone is on the same page throughout the planning process and on the day.

You Are Who You Surround Yourself With (Chapter 9, 10 & 11): You become the average of the people you spend the most time with. Choose them wisely. From your vendors to the family and friends that you involve in the wedding planning, be intentional about who you will be surrounded by and use their strengths and talents to your advantage.

Conflict Management (Chapter 12): When you face conflict, a few distinctions and reframes can be all you need to get what you want without damaging the relationship. The Nonviolent Communication framework is a tool you can use in all areas of life way beyond your wedding planning.

Money (Chapter 13): Money is one of these sensitive topics that most families don't talk about openly. As we grow up, we often carry money wounds and a wedding tends to surface these pretty visibly. Making money a recurring topic of conversation as a couple is one of the healthiest practices you can implement today that will elevate your relationship to new heights, while lowering your stress.

Enjoy Your Wedding Day (Chapter 14): You can plan, prepare and rehearse all you want, on your wedding day most is set and you'll have to go with the flow. Hopefully the flow is aligned to your vision, but if there are unforeseen hiccups along the way, learn to take them with healthy detachment so that you can enjoy your day and your people. Your relationships are the true gems of your life.

Self-Image (Chapter 15): If you don't enjoy being in front of the camera, you're not alone. The best you can do is to choose a great photographer who makes you feel at ease, allows you to be yourself and forget the camera is even here.

You Alone Can Change Your World (Chapter 16): Your surroundings impact you, but it works both ways. When you change, people around you adjust to who you are becoming. Even if your spouse isn't interested in this work, don't let it be the reason why you don't start it yourself.

Stress-free Wedding

What exactly is BLISS by Caroline?

For over a decade, my husband, Jean-Laurent Gaudy (JL) has been a wedding photographer. Over the years he noticed a growing need among his clients for guidance on how to navigate the complexities of their wedding planning with less stress.

Their lives were already hectic and planning a wedding on top of it all could be overwhelming. A few themes kept coming back: budget, family dynamics, self-image challenges...

While wedding planners often strive to assist couples, many lack the specialized training or interest in providing comprehensive emotional support.

JL frequently found himself in a pickle: who could help his clients with stress management on their wedding planning journey?

He had an answer: Me!

He'd been encouraging me to join his venture for a while, praising my ability to connect with people and my passion for relationships. Though I initially hesitated due to my existing executive coaching business, a recent workshop experience changed my mind.

Early Spring 2024, during an 8-week executive coaching program, I dedicated a chapter to relationships. The response was overwhelming. My clients were captivated by the insights I shared, and many expressed how transformative it had been.
Inspired by this, JL again suggested we create a side business together.

And so, BLISS was born.

Our mission at BLISS

BLISS by Caroline (referred to as BLISS in this book) was born from the understanding that wedding planning should be a joyful journey, not a stressful one. Our fast-paced world often leaves us feeling overwhelmed, making it difficult to navigate life's challenges with grace. BLISS is here to change that. By helping you manage stress, I empower you to be your best self throughout the entire wedding planning process, culminating in the unforgettable celebration you deserve.

At BLISS by Caroline you will find mental and emotional support for couples or individuals as they plan their wedding.

How does BLISS by Caroline differ from premarital counseling?

- Premarital counseling is a special form of couples therapy that helps you strengthen your relationship and identify any blind spots prior to getting married. It helps the couple identify their past wounds to make your marriage successful.

- BLISS by Caroline is a coaching support that <u>can be done alone or with your partner</u> and is focused on giving you the tools to plan your wedding with calm and ease. It offers the support to address the challenges you are facing now and throughout your wedding planning journey. Everything you'll learn will help you beyond your wedding and can transform all areas of your life.

That said, you can choose to do both as they are complementary.

How does BLISS work?

At the time of writing this book, we only offer high-touch containers and contents that are bespoke to you and your unique circumstances so that you can navigate your wedding planning stress-free.

The 4 pillars of BLISS

The 4 focus areas that I help my clients with are:

Stress Management - Learn how to reduce overwhelm, regain control over your time, and use delegation intentionally to manage unforeseen circumstances and interference with ease and grace.

Shared Vision & Enjoyment - Align your vision and expectations with each other and with others to ensure the journey to your wedding day is smooth and frictionless.

Strengthened Bond - Ensure that your time preparing for your big day brings you closer, deepens your intimacy and connection to remember this time as fun and joyful.

Heightened Self-Image - Embrace your style unapologetically and get confident in front of the camera and in your body to get the most authentic memories of your wedding day.

That said, as every situation is unique and BLISS is only about bespoke support, I will support you with the topics that are most important to you within or outside these 4 pillars.

Do you want bespoke support to help you as you navigate your wedding planning?

I've got you! I'll be happy to assist you and share resources to help you with your unique circumstances. There are two ways to get in touch:
- Send me an email at book@blissbycaroline.com and tell me more about your situation so I can best support you,
- Use the QR code at the end of the book to schedule a chat with me.

FOREWORD

Our atypical love story

JL and I have been married 10 years (at the time of writing this book); our parents haven't met and they probably never will.

We've been together 15 years and we have a 5-year-old daughter. We are on good terms with our parents. They all live about 3 to 5 hours apart from each other. So there is no real obstacle to their meeting. This was not intentional, but this is our reality.

Our marriage is strong and continues to grow stronger with time. Some of our friends often tell us how lucky we are or ask for guidance on how to recreate such a happy marriage. From the inside we have gone through lots of challenges and change. It's not easy to have a long-lasting, powerful relationship. But it doesn't have to be complicated.

As I reminisce on our wedding planning, the feeling I remember is ease, calm and fun. I hold on to the togetherness and how aligned we were.

It also reminds me of one of the toughest conversations I have ever had in my life: telling my parents and my sister that we were not inviting them. It didn't come from a malicious place at all. At the time of our wedding (which we had to precipitate for immigration timeline reasons) we thought that we were going to get officially married then and would eventually celebrate our union with a party and with friends and family later on.

My family lived far away and it felt unfair (and a waste of time and money) to expect them to travel 12 hours (by plane), pretty last minute, to be there for an one-hour moment with the mayor of our town, right before we would both return to work. JL and I were both aligned to that decision and it also meant that we could not have my in-laws either, even if they lived a few hours away from us (by train).

We held strong and each of us had the conversations we were dreading, twice, as our parents were separated. This unintentional event set something very strong for our marriage: we operate as a team even when it's painful. We know to hold firm on shared decisions and we find a way to overcome any challenge together.

Why I Wrote This Book

I'll be honest, a solid, strong and powerful marriage requires investment. It's not a one-time deal and rather a never-ending commitment.

> *"A successful marriage requires falling in love many times, always with the same person."*
> *- Mignon McLaughlin*

As time passes, you evolve, your spouse too, and sometimes not in the same direction. Making your marriage work will require adjustments, an open-mind, a lot of genuine curiosity and acceptance for who each of you are choosing to become, and a solid commitment to the relationship. Of course, love is fundamental but it doesn't do it all.

I co-founded BLISS with my husband JL (a professional wedding photographer with over a decade experience and international clients) because I have realized how many friends, connections, and clients of his are embarking on their wedding planning with many illusions, only to face some real challenges on their way.

Some look back at their wedding with regrets, others realize that so many of the problems they had in their marriage could have been prevented if they had addressed it before getting married.

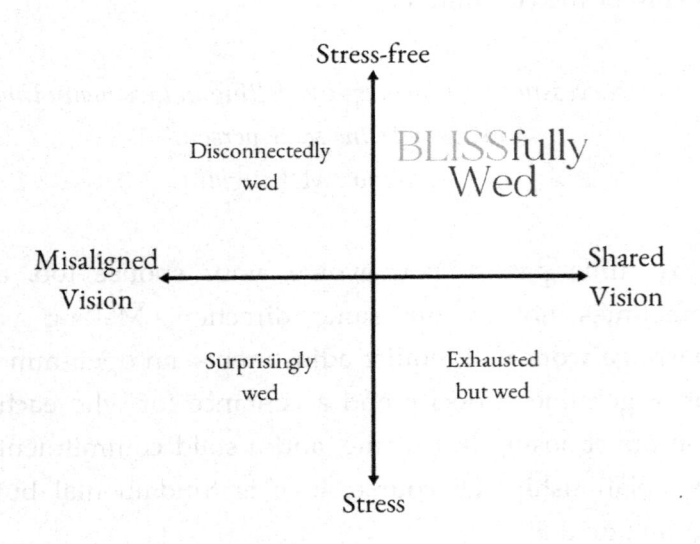

	Stress-free	
Disconnectedly wed		BLISSfully Wed
Misaligned Vision ←		→ Shared Vision
Surprisingly wed		Exhausted but wed
	Stress	

The premise of this book is to help you navigate your wedding planning with low stress, while bringing your common vision to life to not only create a memorable and enjoyable wedding, but to build the foundations for a long-lasting, happy marriage.

My intention with *Stress-free Wedding* is to set you up for success. I can't promise that all will be smooth and I can guarantee that challenges and problems will arise. But I have gathered in this book some of the most powerful ways to make your wedding planning and your wedding day as enjoyable as possible. And the beauty of it is that all these tools will help you forever in your marriage and in all areas of your life.

You don't have to read this book with your partner (I'll be sharing more about this in Chapter 16). You absolutely can, but it works just as well whether you both read it or only one of you does.

This book is aimed at teaching you what - in my opinion - are some of the most vital tools to thrive in life and yet have not made their way to our school system. That said, I intend to make this resource the most practical, simple to use and easy to remember. There are a lot of wonderful books if you want to deep-dive further into some of the concepts I'll be sharing. For now, let's focus on what is at the top of your to-do list: navigating your wedding planning with ease and calm.

The book is divided in 6 sections:

Section 1: Stress Management - Learn how to reduce overwhelm, regain control of your time, and use delegation effectively to manage unexpected challenges with ease and grace.

Section 2: Craft Your Shared Vision - Align your vision and expectations with each other and with others to ensure the journey to your wedding day is smooth and frictionless.

Section 3: Enjoyment Enhancers - Build a dream team, aligned to your vision and ready to support you throughout your wedding planning.

Section 4: Your Biggest Stressors - Learn how to address your biggest sources of stress without risking to ruin your relationship.

Section 5: Your Wedding Day - Prepare for your big day and its potential surprises so that you surf that wave joyfully and with calm, so that you always hold on to the best memories.

Section 6: Your Journey beyond Your Wedding Day - My intention is to help you before, during and after your wedding day. And I want to leave you with closing thoughts on how to best prepare for what's next.

And if you want to dig deeper and get bespoke support with your unique circumstances, let's chat.

Two ways to get in touch with me:
- Send me an email at book@blissbycaroline.com and tell me more about your challenges,
- Use the QR code at the end of the book to schedule a chat with me.

I'll be honored to assist you in any way I can.

Ready? Let's dive in!

Actually, before we do, you have to promise me something. Don't just read this book, put it into practice. I made sure to make it short and actionable so that you can truly transform your wedding planning experience.

You will find **BLISS Coaching Questions** throughout the book to get you into action mode. Don't read and skip the work. Do it!

Promise? Let's go.

SECTION 1
Stress Management

SECTION 1
Stress Management

CHAPTER 1

It's Not What You Think

You're in love. You're engaged. The world is a magical, shimmering place. You're planning a wedding. And you're losing your mind.

Let's be honest. The lead-up to your wedding day is a whirlwind of emotions, expectations, and, let's face it, a whole lot of stress. You're probably caught in a loop of social media perfection, family opinions, and a never-ending to-do list that seems to grow by the minute. It's easy to get caught up in the details – the dress, the venue, the flowers – and believe that these are the things causing you stress. But here's a little secret: they're not.

The real culprit behind your wedding-induced anxiety is much deeper. It's the pressure to create a flawless day, the fear of disappointing loved ones, and the overwhelming sense of uncertainty about what comes next.

Before we get practical on how to tell your mother-in-law to stay out of the way in a fashion that won't start a generational trauma for your family, let's start at the beginning, shall we?

And it begins with your mind.

I know, I know... it might sound totally boring or downright offensive, but hear me out. I promise I'm on your team!

I know what you're thinking: *"But I don't care about my mind, I'm stressed about the seating chart!"* Trust me, I get it. The seating chart is a nightmare. But it's not the root of your problem. It's a symptom. A symptom of a larger issue: our lack of education on how to manage stress effectively.

If I was to pour salt on your beautiful and healthy arm, you would at best not feel anything and at worse find it ticklish, right?

Now if I was doing the exact same thing on your arm with a deep open wound, you'd possibly yell of pain.

If it hurts, it's not healed.

In this analogy, salt is the stressor. And as you can understand, salt is not the problem.

Whatever is causing you stress on your wedding planning journey is salt. The timeline, the in-laws, the budget... all of it is like salt. And it gives you a powerful indicator of how healed you are from your own wounds. And yes, we all have some.

But let me make something crystal clear right now: NOTHING is wrong with you. Welcome to being a human!

The moment you understand and accept your own contribution to your stress, everything becomes easier and will start making more sense.

Stress-free Wedding

CHAPTER 2

Your Mind: The Wedding Crasher

You've probably heard the expression, "You are what you eat." But what about "You are how you think"?

Let's talk about your mind. Not the kind of mind that's brilliant at math or witty in social situations. We're talking about your subconscious, the part of you that runs the show without you even realizing it.

The truth is, you're not your mind. Your mind is a tool, like a car. You're the driver. And just like a car, your mind can be a powerful ally or a total pain in the neck. The key is to learn how to drive it.

Your mind is a tool, like a car. You're the driver.

Now, your mind has a bit of a negativity bias (the majority of our thoughts are negative). It's like a pessimist who's convinced a rainstorm is coming no matter how sunny it is outside... It's always on the lookout for threats, always ready to protect you. That's great when you're facing a saber-tooth tiger, but not so much when you're dealing with selecting a wedding photographer - by the way if you haven't done so already check out my husband's portfolio (www.jeanlaurentgaudy.com) and get this task done already. Just saying ;).

Your mind is also more interested in survival than thriving. It's concerned with keeping you alive, not with making you happy. So, when you're planning a wedding, your mind might be more focused on potential disasters than on creating beautiful memories.

And here's the kicker: how you experience stress is directly tied to your mind. When your mind is in overdrive, everything feels magnified. A small hiccup becomes a catastrophe. A minor disagreement feels like World War III.

So, what can you do? Well, that's what this first section is all about. But for now, just remember: you're not alone.

Millions of people are battling their minds every day. And the good news is, with a little understanding and practice, you can take back the wheel.

Let's dive deeper into how your mind works and why it's sabotaging your wedding planning bliss.

First, imagine having a puppy. Let's call this puppy Max. Max is cute and adorable and it's untrained. So when it needs to pee, Max will just pee wherever it stands. Same for poop. If you decided to let Max figure out life on its own it will probably pee and poop all over your house day after day, right? You could also decide to train it and teach Max where it is acceptable and appropriate to pee and poop. It's also probably clear in your mind, if you've ever had a dog, that the longer you wait until you decide to train the dog, the harder it will be for Max to unlearn a well established habit of peeing on your favorite shoes and to integrate the fact that now it's no longer an option. Correct?

Your mind is like Max. For most of our lives, we have not been told that we needed to tame our minds. And now that we do, it's like unlearning and relearning a completely different way of living our lives. But trust me, it's so worth it!

Your Conscious versus Subconscious Mind

- **The Autopilot Mode - Your Subconscious:** Your subconscious is like that amazing autopilot feature in your car. It handles routine tasks without you even thinking about them. It's responsible for habits, emotions, and bodily functions. It's also where your beliefs and values reside. This is the part of your brain that's creating those stress responses without you even realizing it.

- **The Conscious Captain - You:** You're the CEO of your mind. You have the power to override your autopilot and make conscious choices. This is where mindfulness and self-awareness come in. It's like learning to drive a manual car - more effort at first, but greater control in the long run.

How Your Brain Works

- **The Negative Nancy - Your Brain's Bias:** Your brain is naturally wired to focus on the negative. It's a survival mechanism. If you were constantly thinking about all the good things in life, you might forget to look out for that saber-tooth tiger. But in today's world, this negativity bias can be a real buzzkill. It's like wearing negative-tinted glasses. Everything looks a bit gloomier than it really is.

- **The Fight or Flight Friend - Your Stress Response:** Your body has an incredible ability to respond to danger. It's called the fight-or-flight response. When you perceive a threat (like a looming wedding deadline), your body releases hormones that prepare you for action. But in today's world, most of our "threats" are mental, not physical. That said, our mind doesn't distinguish between the two and treats them equally as life threatening. So, that extra energy gets stored as tension, anxiety, or even physical symptoms.

Understanding these basic principles of psychology is the first step to taking control of your mind and reducing wedding stress.

How do you become the captain of your mind? Before we talk about that, I want to explore with you in the next chapter what happens when you experience stress.

CHAPTER 3

Stress: The Uninvited Guest

Stress. We all know it's there, but do we really understand it? It's that pesky uninvited guest who shows up at your wedding planning party, draining the joy and making everyone uncomfortable. And no, I didn't say Uncle Rob, who always has an inappropriate joke to share with the world on his social media, or your cousin Tess, whose depressive whinnies are now famously known by all... I said Stress ;).

Picture this: It's the morning of your big day. You're surrounded by loved ones, hair and makeup are perfection on Earth, and you're feeling like a million bucks. Then, the unthinkable happens: the florist calls to say the entire flower order has been delivered to a cat convention.

Panic sets in. Your mind races faster than a caffeinated squirrel on a treadmill. Your heart pounds like a hummingbird on steroids. You're suddenly channeling your inner superhero, brainstorming solutions at warp speed. This is your body's way of saying, "Hey, something's up! Let's get ready to pounce (or, you know, find some replacement flowers)."

Just like a caveman who saw a hungry lion ready to eat him for breakfast, your body is primed for action. But instead of dodging prehistoric predators, you're dodging a floral fiasco.

Stress is your body's natural response to perceived threats. Let's dissect what happens to you physiologically when faced with such a wedding nightmare.

Stress Cycle: The Wedding Edition

Stress isn't just a Monday morning grump or a pre-wedding panic attack. It's more like a persistent, uninvited guest who shows up at your door, refuses to leave, and starts making a mess. This pesky party crasher follows a pretty predictable routine.

First, there's the *trigger*. This is when life throws you a curveball – like getting that call from your florist. This curveball jolts you out of your zen zone and into "fight or flight" mode (essentially a state of survival as if the situation was a life or death matter).

Next comes the *response*. Your body goes into full-on panic mode. Heart racing, palms sweating, and a sudden urge to eat an entire pint of ice cream – it's like your body is hosting its own personal rave without inviting you.

Finally, there's the *recovery*. Once the initial shock wears off, your body starts to calm down. It's like the party's over, and you're left to clean up the mess. This is where you can start to rebuild your zen and get back to enjoying your wedding day.

The problem with the stress cycle is that most people never close the loop. They stay on trigger-response mode non stop and live in a state of chronic stress.

Stress and Your Mind

Your mind is a powerful tool, but it can also be your worst enemy when it comes to stress. When stress strikes, our minds go into overdrive. It's like trying to juggle chainsaws while riding a unicycle - chaotic and overwhelming.

Our focus narrows, tuning out everything except the stressful situation. We might experience racing thoughts, difficulty concentrating, and even memory lapses. Our problem-solving skills can go out the window as our brains become fixated on the perceived threat. It's like our minds have been hijacked by a tiny, panicky dictator, shouting orders and ignoring reason.

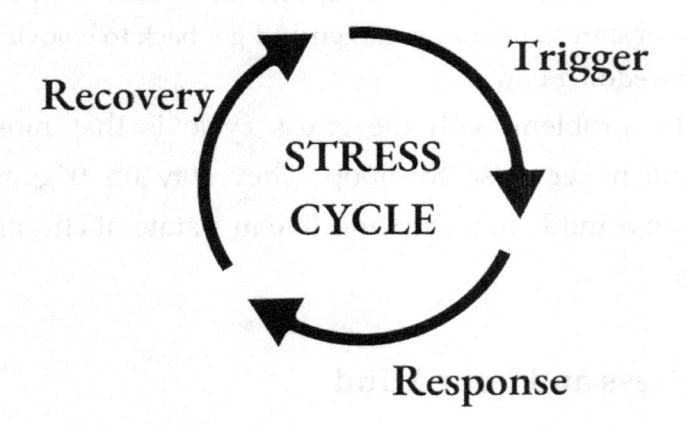

STRESS CYCLE

Recovery → Trigger → Response → Recovery

Stress cycle: A trigger creates a stress response. Until you close the loop of stress and return to homeostasis, your mind and body stay on alert mode.

Stress and Your Body

Your body is a complex machine, and stress can throw it out of whack. When you're stressed, your body releases hormones like cortisol and adrenaline. When overly secreted, these hormones can cause physical symptoms like headaches, muscle tension, digestive problems, and weakened immune system.

Stress and Your Perception

Stress distorts your perception of reality. You experience selective hearing and tunnel vision, all in that pursuit to be hyper effective while running away from the tiger and often without even realizing it. You might find yourself being overly critical, impatient, or reactive. Stress can also affect your relationships, as you might take out your frustrations on those closest to you.

Alright! You've officially graduated from Stress 101. Now you know how stress affects your mind and body.

Next, let's delve into practical strategies to help you and your partner navigate the stressful waters of wedding planning.

CHAPTER 4

Taming the Wedding Stress Monster

So, you've identified the stress cycle. Now, you're left with a choice. You can let stress dominate your life or you can take control and regain your power, get back on the driver's seat and control it.

Hopefully you are nodding at the latter because I have some practical tools to share with you so that you can conquer it. Think of these as your secret weapons against the wedding stress monster (and by all means, everywhere else - not only weddings).

Understand Your Stressors

The first step is to identify what's causing you the most stress. Is it the guest list, the budget, or dealing with family drama? Once you know your enemy, you can strategize accordingly. But remember my salt story earlier? Keep in mind that the only way to navigate your wedding planning (and life) with ease and calm is to get to the root causes of your stress. Unearthing the reasons why your mother-in-law gets under your skin so easily or why the thought of a to-do list gives you panic attacks can transform your life.

Until then, addressing the symptoms can do miracles but only in the short-term.

Communicate Openly

Talk to your partner about your stress levels. Sharing your feelings can be incredibly relieving. You might find that you're both feeling overwhelmed by the same things. Open communication is the foundation of a strong relationship, and it's especially important during stressful times.

For example, I have a practice. When I wake up, the first thing I do is check how I feel. If I'm fully rested and energized I go on with my day. If I don't feel refreshed or have had a short or challenging night I inform my husband and daughter that I am not at my best, which means I may not be as patient, I may be more irritated, and that it has nothing to do with them. I make the request that everyone acknowledges my state and ask them to be empathetic with me that day. The result is magical!

RED: The Non-negotiable

There are 3 things you must prioritize to help lower your stress level. I call it the RED (Rest, Exercise, Diet).

Rest: Sleep is the most underrated stress management tool. Getting good quality and enough sleep on a regular basis will allow the best version of yourself to surface. Which, in turn, amplifies your most beautiful relationships.

I was severely sleep deprived for two and a half years when our daughter was young, and I remember how everything felt hard and overwhelming. The moment she slept through the night and I was able to rest, my entire life felt easier and more enjoyable. My relationship with my husband grew to levels I never thought possible, my entire life felt exciting again and even my career skyrocketed.

Did you know that top athletes incorporate rest & recovery in their high-performance training plans? Four-time NBA MVP player, LeBron James sleeps at least 8 to 10 hours every night, and so does tennis legend Roger Federer, Usain Bolt, Venus Williams, Maria Sharapova and Steve Nash. If wedding planning doesn't feel like high performance sports yet, give it a few weeks and then apply the techniques of the GOATs.

Struggling with your sleep? Here are rules you can start implementing to improve the duration and quality of your sleep (which should solve most of your sleep challenges):

- Set a bedtime and stick to it.
- 10 hours before bed, no caffeine.
- 3 hours before bed, no food.
- 2 hours before bed, no work.
- 1 hour before bed, no screens.
- In bed, use the Navy Seals 4-7-8 Breathing method or a body scan meditation.

> 🎥 *I have recorded a short video explaining the Navy Seals 4-7-8 breathing method for you to use. Scan the QR code at the end of the book to access all the bonuses (this one included).*

Exercise: Being intentional about physical activity even if it's not an intense long workout is hugely beneficial (says the woman who just spent an entire day writing a few chapters of this book).

Get out and take a walk! For a bigger impact on your stress level, you want to break a sweat and/or elevate your heartbeat.

The great bonus with exercising is that it helps improve your sleep.

Do you find it hard to squeeze a workout during the day? Try this:
- Find 1 minute a day and do a plank.

Why 1 minute and why the plank? Because every one can find 1 minute per day for anything. So you essentially have 0 excuses ;) And 1 minute of any exercise may not break a sweat which means you can do it in your work clothes, you don't need a full outfit. Planks build core muscles, improve posture and balance, reduce lower back pain, and flatten the stomach (among other benefits).

Diet: Your gut and your brain are BFFs. Believe it or not, what you eat can greatly affect how you feel. When you fill your plate with yummy, healthy foods, it's like giving your body and mind a big hug. This can help calm those wedding planning jitters and keep you feeling good. Think of it as nourishing your soul from the inside out.

So, next time you're stressed about the guest list or the perfect cake, reach for something good for you. Your body and mind will thank you!

Resilience building stress reduction

To the RED list, I like to add 2 resilience building habits that have huge benefits to your overall mental health

Mindfulness: First, let's clarify what mindfulness actually means. Mindfulness is simply being fully present in the moment. It's like pausing your life movie and really soaking in what's happening right now, without getting caught up in worries about the past or future. It's about focusing on an object of attention.

Meditation is one of many mindfulness practices. It comes with lots of preconceived ideas. That's why I teach a 1-minute meditation to my clients to show them how beneficial it is even for 60 seconds.

Using breath work is another great way to reduce your stress response. It is socially acceptable and easy to use without anyone noticing it.

I have recorded a short video with my go-to breathing technique for you to use. Scan the QR code at the end of the book to access it.

I am a horseback rider and I practice dressage (what people refer to as dancing with a horse). When I ride, there is no room in my mind for anything other than riding. I have to pay attention to my surroundings to not crash into another horse. I think about the next movement I want my horse to perform and therefore the series of cues I have to give it with my body. I pay attention to how it responds to adjust my cues…etc. If you too have a hobby or something you enjoy doing that has you completely focused on that, it's a wonderful mindfulness practice that you want to intentionally add to your days, or as often as you can.

Cold therapy: Cold therapy is like giving your body a refreshing shock. It's when you expose yourself to cold temperatures, whether it's a cold shower, an ice bath, or even just splashing cold water on your face. It might sound intense, but it can help your body feel energized, reduce inflammation, and even boost your mood.

Here are 2 simple ways to use cold therapy:
1. End your shower with a few seconds of cold water and gradually lengthen the time.
2. Icy water on your face in the morning offers stress relief and additional anti-aging benefits.

The Fun Ways To Lower Your Stress

If you practice the REDs on a daily basis and sprinkle some of the resilience building ones when possible, you will see your entire life experience change. The people around you will notice how different you are and may ask for your secret. If they do, I'd be immensely grateful if you mentioned this book ;).

There are some fun and exciting ways to better manage stress that you don't want to miss.

Humans are social creatures, and connection is our lifeline. Spending time with loved ones can be a powerful antidote to stress. When you share your feelings and experiences with others, it can lighten your emotional load. Laughter, shared experiences, and mutual support can create a sense of belonging and security, which are essential for managing stress. Plus, talking to friends or family can offer fresh perspectives and practical advice, helping you feel less overwhelmed.

Sex is nature's stress reliever (and counts triple). It's more than just physical pleasure; it's a powerful way to connect with your partner on a deep level and be fully present. When you get intimate, your body releases feel-good hormones like oxytocin and endorphins, which help to melt away stress and tension. Sex also often rhymes with sweating and elevated heartbeat, which helps with toxin elimination. Isn't stress reduction exciting?

Physical touch is like a warm hug for your soul. It's a powerful stress reliever that can calm your mind and body. When you're touched, your brain releases oxytocin, often called the "love hormone," which helps reduce stress and anxiety. Holding hands, hugging, or cuddling with your partner can create a sense of safety and connection, which can work wonders for your mental well-being.

According to the Gottman Institute, a 6-second kiss (the French way) or a 20-second hug releases oxytocin (the "love" hormone) for both you and your partner and is a wonderful daily practice that not only will alleviate the impact of stress but also create a sense of connection and bonding. It's yet another great way to practice mindfulness.

Don't stress about your stress.

Just remember that it's natural and okay to feel stressed. The key is to manage it effectively so it doesn't consume you. By implementing these strategies, you can navigate the wedding planning process with more ease and enjoyment.

Before we proceed to our next section, here's a last thought for you that can dramatically reduce your stress: delegation.

Delegating Tasks and Responsibilities

Enlisting the help of trusted friends and family can alleviate some of the planning stress.
- **Identify Strengths:** Determine who has the skills and time to assist with specific tasks.
- **Clear Assignments:** Provide clear guidelines and expectations for delegated responsibilities.
- **Show Appreciation:** Express gratitude for their support and contributions.

By carefully selecting and nurturing relationships with your vendors, family and friends and effectively delegating tasks, you'll create a strong foundation for a seamless and enjoyable planning process.

To help you with that, you get to reflect using your first BLISS Coaching Question.

BLISS Coaching Question: Here are 3 powerful questions you can always return to:
1. Does this have to be done right now?
2. Does this have to be done by me?
3. Is there someone who can do this task equally well, if not better than me?

Before we get to the juicy part, where you and your spouse get to envision your ideal celebration, I want to share more about your beliefs and how they are shaping your reality and affect your ability to envision your dream wedding.

SECTION 2
Crafting Your Shared Vision

CHAPTER 5

Your Brain is a Party Animal (With Some Questionable Guests)

So, you've mastered the art of taming the wedding stress monster, huh? Good for you! But let's dig a little deeper. It's time to talk about the architect of your reality: your brain. Yep this one, again!

Think of your brain as a party animal. It loves a good shindig, and it's constantly inviting new guests to the party. Some guests are awesome – funny, intelligent, and bring great snacks. Others? Well, they're more like those relatives who always start a political argument.

These party guests are what we call "beliefs." They're the ideas and opinions that shape how you see the world. They're the reasons you think chocolate cake is the best dessert, that Mondays are terrible, and that wedding planning should be a 24/7 job.

But here's the kicker: your brain is *terrible* at vetting guests. It lets in anyone, from the wise old sage to the delusional conspiracy theorist. And once they're in, it's hard to kick them out.

So, how do you decide which beliefs to keep and which to toss out? That's where the fun begins. Because guess what? You're not stuck with the party guests your brain originally invited. You're the ultimate party planner, and you have the power to decide who stays and who goes.

There is not one reality or one truth. There is only the one you choose to believe in.

My belief building story about success

My parents were entrepreneurs. My mom was a pharmacist and my dad a jack-of-all-trades who worked as a lifeguard, a restaurant and club owner, a general contractor and I'm sure I'm forgetting some of his many ventures.

My mom followed a very traditional straightforward path to success. She grew and scaled her business for 4 decades and sold it for 7 figures when she decided to retire.

As for my dad, that was another story. I'm pretty sure he exited all of his jobs with less money than when he started them. He filed for bankruptcy when I was a teenager. And if it wasn't for their prenup I'm not sure where I would be today.

My dad passed away a few years ago. At his funeral the priest came to me and my sisters asking how we would describe him. My sisters couldn't say a thing. As for me, the answer was crystal clear and I said "Our dad had so many lives in his lifetime. He followed his passion and ideas and unapologetically moved on to the next. He was a happy man because he always did whatever he wanted and always found a way to fall back onto his two feet."

It poured out of me without hesitation. And that's been a moment of a profound realization for me.

You see until that moment I had always considered my mom to be successful and my dad to be a failure. And when I listened to my own spiel about my dad, I realized that they were both successful in their own ways.

Society and the media have been advertising that success means money, status, and limited mistakes (among a long list of dos and don'ts). And for almost 40 years I have fallen in the same trap.

But here's the truth: my mom hated to go to work, to manage employees, or to deal with clients' crises. She suffered from undiagnosed depression, and chronic insomnia all her adult life. She had low self-confidence, and a list of limiting beliefs about her appearance and her abilities. She also ran her business masterfully well, especially considering her mental and emotional health.

My dad slept like a baby, enjoyed the many pleasures of being alive, constantly connected with people, traveled, took risks, and followed his gut all his life. He had unshakeable certainty even after his many business failures. I'm sure he left this world feeling appeased. But he was also an absentee husband and father.

The reason why I'm sharing this with you is this: there is not one reality or one truth. There is only the one you choose to believe in.

"Everything is theoretically impossible, until it is done."
-Robert A. Heinlein

Let's look at two more situations where belief was overturned and gave birth to a radical shift in perspective.

Breaking the Unbreakable: Kipchoge's Sub-Two-Hour Marathon

For decades, the two-hour marathon was considered an impossible feat, a mythical barrier beyond human capacity. The distance, 26.2 miles, was a daunting challenge, and the idea of covering it in less than two hours seemed like the stuff of dreams. Yet, in a stunning display of human endurance and athleticism, Eliud Kipchoge shattered this long-held belief.

In 2019, Kipchoge ran a marathon in Vienna, Austria, finishing in an astonishing time of 1:59:40.2. This groundbreaking achievement defied conventional wisdom and pushed the boundaries of what was thought possible for the human body.

Rewiring the Brain: The Power of Neuroplasticity

For centuries, the human brain was perceived as a static organ, hardwired and unchanging after a critical developmental period. This rigid view held that intelligence, personality, and abilities were fixed at a young age, and decline was inevitable with advancing years. The notion of a brain that could be reshaped, rewired, and optimized was unthinkable.

However, the emergence of neuroplasticity has revolutionized our understanding of the brain. This groundbreaking concept reveals that the brain is remarkably adaptable, capable of forming new neural connections, and reorganizing itself throughout life. It's as if the brain possesses an innate ability to learn, grow, and change, much like a muscle.

What was once considered a biological destiny is now understood as an opportunity for transformation. Neuroplasticity has challenged the limitations imposed by age, injury, and even genetics. From stroke survivors regaining lost functions to individuals learning new skills at advanced ages, the power of the brain to reshape itself is continually inspiring.

Your Brain's Belief Factory

Think of beliefs as those old, familiar songs that get stuck in your head. You've heard them a million times, and they're comfortable, even if they're a bit of an ear worm.

Beliefs are basically ideas about how the world works, what's possible, and what's not. They're formed from a mix of your experiences, what you've been taught, and what you've observed. It's like your brain is a sponge, soaking up information from your environment.

For example, if you grew up hearing that "weddings are stressful," your brain might start to believe it's a universal truth. Or, if you saw a lot of lavish weddings on social media, you might believe that your wedding needs to be just as extravagant. These beliefs become your mental blueprint, shaping how you see the world and how you respond to situations.

But here's the thing: just because you believe something doesn't mean it's true. Your brain is great at creating stories, but it's not always accurate. So, it's time to question your party guests and decide who gets to stay and who needs to leave.

Where Do These Beliefs Come From?

Family Influence: The Original Party Crashers

Your family introduces you to the world, and their beliefs become the foundation of your own. You have accepted their beliefs to be true and these thoughts have been on your mind for so long that you've not been questioning them.

Society's Guest List: The Popular Crowd
Society is another big belief machine that has been feeding us so many thoughts through the media, our friends, and even strangers. It's like scrolling through Instagram and thinking everyone's life is perfect. It can be a lot of fun, but deep down we also know it may not be the whole picture.

Personal Experiences: The Uninvited Guests
Life is full of surprises, and some of them crash your brain party without an invitation. Heartbreaks, triumphs, and everything in between shape your beliefs. It's like learning a tough lesson and vowing never to repeat it. These experiences can be powerful, but they can also create some pretty stubborn beliefs.

Your brain is constantly adding new beliefs, and some old ones might sneak out the back door. The key is to become discerning and choose the ones who contribute to your happiness and well-being.

CHAPTER 6

Your Beliefs: The Secret Sauce (or Saboteur) of Your Relationship

Once you understand that what you have been believing until now may not be the absolute truth and that you can upgrade your thoughts to create new beliefs that serve you, let's briefly close that important tangent I took to see why upgrading your beliefs is fundamental.

Repeated thoughts

↘ ↓ ↙

| Beliefs |
| Perspective |
| Action |
| Result |

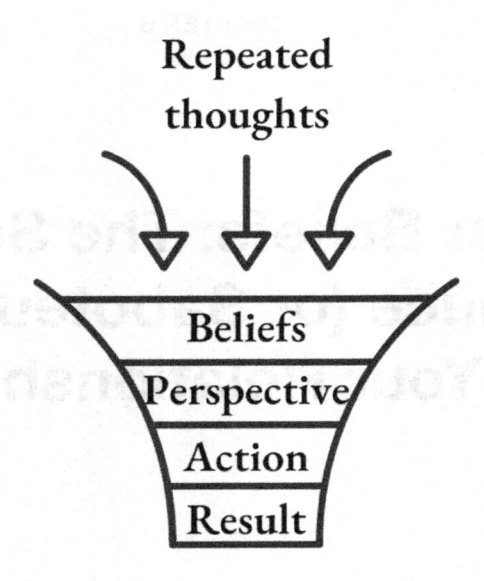

Thoughts that you repeat or that you hear repeatedly become beliefs. Beliefs then create your perspective on your world, which informs your actions and directly impacts your results. If you want different outcomes, upgrade your beliefs.

Beliefs shape your perception. How you see your partner, your relationship, and the world around you is filtered through your belief system.

Beliefs drive your actions. Your beliefs influence how you behave and the actions you take.

Beliefs create results. Your behavior and actions result in your outcomes.

My point is that everyone and their father (why pick on moms all the time?) have told you what to believe, what was "true" and acceptable and it has shaped your view of the world. And these inherited beliefs might have gotten in the way of your wedding planning.

Upgrading Your Beliefs

BLISS Coaching Question: Imagine you're at your wedding day and for some unfortunate set of circumstances you are told in the morning that no one but your partner and the vendors will show up. 0 guests. What are the things you are planning that you would enjoy 100% even if no one was watching?

You don't have to do something "because that's how it's done". Do it because you really want it and you would still really want it if no one was here to witness it.

Personally, I would still love to look and feel stunning. I would most likely choose a color that fits my skin tone and I'm pretty sure white is not it. I would definitely enjoy the food, the dance, and the flowers. I would still love to prepare guest party favors even if no one took them.

Get to the core of what you really enjoy and give yourself permission to bend the rules. Because it's YOUR day. And as always, align your ideas with your partner.

Changing your beliefs takes time and repetition. Doing it alone is particularly challenging because we have blind spots. Outside perspective from an expert will fast track your progress and will make your hard work so rewarding. Whatever you decide, be patient with yourself and celebrate small victories.

I've recorded a short video to help you further with changing your beliefs. Use the QR code on the last page of this book to access it.

Stress-Colored Glasses

Imagine your brain is a camera. Under normal circumstances, it captures the world in vibrant, high-definition color. But when stress kicks in, it's like someone's slapped a pair of sepia-toned sunglasses on the lens. Everything looks duller, grainier, and a whole lot more dramatic.

Stress has a sneaky way of distorting our perception of reality. It's like looking at the world through a funhouse mirror; everything seems bigger, smaller, or just plain weird. Small problems become insurmountable mountains, and minor inconveniences turn into full-blown catastrophes.

Ever caught yourself spiraling about a tiny mistake, only to realize later it wasn't that big of a deal? That's your stress-colored glasses at work. It's like your brain is playing a cruel joke on you, turning up the volume on negativity and muting the joy.

This distorted view of the world can wreak havoc on your relationships, your job, and your overall happiness. It's like walking through life with a permanent case of the Mondays. But the good news is, you can take off those stress-colored glasses. By managing stress effectively (as shown earlier) you can restore your vision and see the world in clearer, more vibrant colors.

You create your own reality. There is no one truth, there is the one you choose to believe. Hopefully, after discovering more about beliefs you are choosing those that serve you and make you happy, regardless of how acceptable they are to others.

CHAPTER 7

Your Wedding, Your Way: Designing Your Dream Day

Let's face it, weddings can turn into a whirlwind of Pinterest perfection and societal expectations. But amidst the chaos, it's easy to forget that your wedding is *your* love story, not a carbon copy of someone else's. It's time to take the reins and create a celebration that truly reflects *you* as a couple.

But there is no "we" if there is no "me". And as you now know, a lot of what you have believed to be absolutely true, may not be. You can upgrade your beliefs to new ones that serve you and your love story.

Less Perfect, More Real

We're constantly bombarded with images of flawless weddings, but perfection is a myth. The most memorable celebrations are often those that feel authentic and genuine. By embracing imperfections and letting go of unrealistic expectations, you'll create a wedding that's truly yours and unforgettable for all the right reasons.

People won't remember your wedding dress, your flowers or your venue, they will remember how your wedding day felt.

Lost in the Wedding Noise

One of the biggest hurdles couples face is drowning in the sea of wedding trends and expectations. It's like trying to find your voice in a crowded room full of shouting matchmakers. You start to question your own desires and what really matters.

Before you and your partner surface your shared vision for your big day, you need to know individually what that vision looks like. Then you can share with each other and have deep, insightful conversations together to align your visions together.

To do so, I'm going to walk you through a series of fun exercises to help you unearth your vision. For each exercise, <u>do it on your own first</u> (without considering what you know your partner would like or prefer; you only want to connect to your desires alone), before sharing what came up for you with your partner.

I'm sharing a few exercises to provoke your thinking differently each time and also because, in my experience, each person can resonate with one tool over the other. For that reason I highly encourage you to do them all, this way you'll have a larger and broader perspective on your vision.

Before we dive in, there are 2 rules that you must follow:
1. Don't try to answer this question in your head. Take a piece of paper out and write it down, or type a note on your phone. This is very important.
2. Another crucial rule is no censor. Don't try to make sense of what comes up, don't judge it either. Just write with as many vivid details that come to mind.

Ready? Let's go!

Sole decision-maker

First, I'd like you to consider this first question and write all of what comes to mind. Use a timer and give yourself 3 minutes.

> **BLISS Coaching Question:** Imagine being the sole decision-maker. What would your wedding look like if money & time were no object and societal expectations didn't exist?

By stripping away the constraints and your inherited beliefs, you can uncover your true desires. This exercise will help you prioritize what truly matters and create a wedding that's an authentic reflection of your love story.

Write down <u>everything</u> that you thought about, even if it seems insignificant, silly, inappropriate or impossible.

Take a moment and share with your partner what was your experience and what scenes or feelings you had. If there was anything surprising or unexpected, share it with them. It's a lovely way to connect at a much deeper level with your lover.

If you want to go further, scan the QR code on the last page of the book for a 5-minute powerful guided creative visualization I have recorded to help you use a different level of consciousness to answer the question. You can listen to it alone or as a couple.

Remember to journal on what comes up without filtering anything out when you're done with the visualization exercise. Then, take a moment and share with your partner what was your experience and what scenes or feelings you had. If there was anything surprising or unexpected, share it with them. It's a lovely way to connect at a much deeper level with your lover.

Your intentions

Next, I'm inviting you to fill out the statements below. Remember, do it alone first and then share your answers with your spouse to compare what came up for each of you.

BLISS Coaching Questions: You can get additional insights by finishing the below prompts.

The 3 words that best describe my wedding are: ...., ..., ...

I want to remember my wedding day as the most...

At my wedding I want to feel ...., ..., ... (Choose 3 feelings - you can use the Wheel of Emotions below.)

I want my family and friends to remember my wedding day as the most/best ....

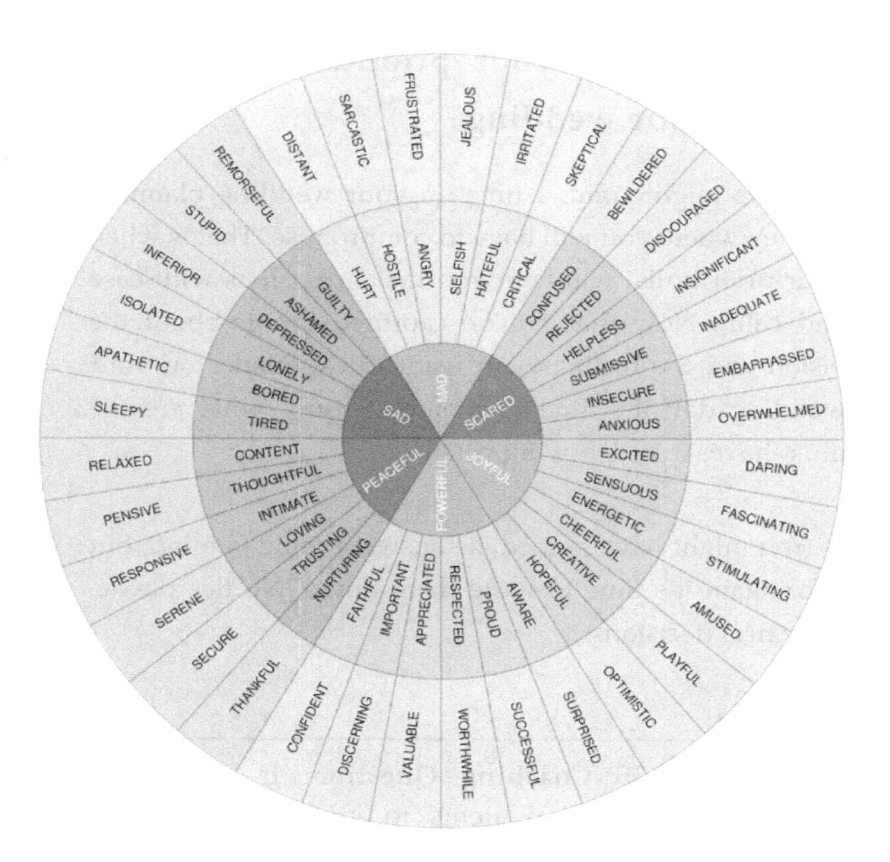

Wheel of emotions - Gloria Cox

The goal here is not to compromise or have similar answers to your partner. It is simply to acknowledge what is most important for each of you.

Get clear on your priorities and must-haves for the wedding

There might come a time on your wedding planning journey where you will have to compromise. That is when your priority list will help you make decisions with ease and calm. Now that you've captured inputs about the vision and the feelings you want to experience on your wedding day it's time to identify clearly what are the must-haves in order of importance.

You might have immediate answers come to mind, but once again it's time to write them down. No ties please. Only firm decisions!

BLISS Coaching Question: If you were allowed only 5 items to invest in for your wedding day what would they be?

Here's another fun activity to do with your spouse! Do it separately first and then discuss your answers together.

If I had to answer this question, I'd say:
1. Caterer
2. Photography
3. Flowers
4. Bridal designer
5. Hair & make up

I love food. Nothing makes me more excited than a delicious healthy meal with my husband.

I want memories that last forever. In my day-to-day I snap pictures constantly. My wedding day would be no exception.

I also have a passion for flowers (to the point of investing in a flower arrangement course a few years ago). Flowers change the energy of a room and affect mine in the best way possible.

And well, if I want these memories to look stunning on pictures I'd definitely want to have an outfit that makes me feel at my best and some help with my hair and make-up because that's not something I master.

As you see, for me the venue is not as important because I can imagine getting married in a meadow, on picnic mats. I would probably get married bare feet, too. Because that's just who I am.

Now it's your turn.

Write your answers down and reflect on the reasons why you picked these. And then share it with your partner. The goal here is not to make your 5 items match. It is to have an insightful conversation. Maybe your spouse will challenge your items because they know you well and will help you refine your list with something you forgot. Maybe you 2 will have similar answers or totally different ones. It's all good!

My tip to bulletproof your list: When you have your final list in order, ask yourself if I could only have 1 thing for my wedding would my first choice really make me happy? Then add the second, and go through the same question. And do so with all 5 to be clear on your priorities.

How To Use That List

Hold on to that list, as it will become instrumental for the rest of your wedding planning.

Put it All Together

There is no right or wrong way to bring all these elements together to form your vision. I'm a fan of visual boards and I like them to be printed. If you are sound-driven, like my husband, you can find different media (something like a video collage or a playlist to embody how you want to feel) to represent your vision and priorities in a way that can be shared with others and understood by them.

You can do it however you prefer. If you need some inspiration, you can start categorizing all of your thoughts and insights from the previous exercises using sensorial and emotional filters:

Visual (colors, space, time of day)
Olfactory (fragrance)
Gustatory (flavors)
Auditive (sounds, music)
Tactile (texture)
Emotional (feelings)
Connective (the people and their vibe)

I've compiled some examples to spark your imagination on the bonus page. Scan the QR Code on the last page of the book to access it.

Note: I would love to see what you came up with. Send me what you created by email at: book@blissbycaroline.com. I read all of your messages.

Share and align the vision with your partner

The big moment has arrived. The time where "me" becomes "we". To make it even more fun you can organize a date where each of you will reveal their vision.

A few warnings first.

This time is not a moment to criticize or to try to win over your future spouse. It's an important step to getting to know and love each other even more. It's a moment where we embrace our differences and welcome them as complementary.

Your unique vision is like your creative baby. You don't want someone to tell you your baby's ears are funny or that their smile is crooked, right? That's why you will honor your lover's vision as much as you want yours respected.

As I was saying earlier, not all exercises will resonate the same for each of you. Maybe your partner could only feel comfortable finishing the prompts. Or maybe they are not visual and they prefer writing their vision, while you will come with a vision board with pictures and scents. Have no expectations and no judgment. If you spend days putting your board together, printing pictures from the color printer at work, afraid to be caught using professional resources for your personal life, getting out of your way to make it all awesome, and they come with 3 lines on a piece of paper, that does not mean they are not taking it seriously.

It only means that you were more inspired, or maybe more creative than they are.

Give your partner some grace and appreciate that they joined you for that date and important step in your wedding planning.

Grace, respect, honor, open-mindedness, no expectations… just love and ready for a nice time together. Promise?

So What Now?

Great! Now, let's delve into what you want to get out of this shared vision date.

You want to come out of this moment (and maybe moments if it becomes too overwhelming or you decide to split it across a few dates & conversations) with a sense that both of you will have the wedding they want. It's the time where "my vision" and "your vision" becomes "our vision".

Different scenarios may come. Let's look at each of them in more detail, shall we?

Scenario 1: Your visions match perfectly

It's very unlikely but not impossible that you are 100% aligned. Your priorities are the same, both your visions were so close it's unbelievable, the words you each used were congruent. In which case your job is easy and done.

Scenario 2: Your visions were aligned on the most important things with some minors differences

If you feel like the compromises you need to make are minor and not that high in your priority list, settle right there what you are both deciding. Redo your vision boards or documents to align exactly on what you both agree to.

Scenario 3: Your visions somewhat align but there are some important elements that don't match

It's important to get curious about what each of you want and why. Why are you so set on a religious ceremony when you haven't gone to church since you were 7 years old and your partner is atheist? It's just as important to get curious about your partner's priorities. Why do they want their mother as an officiant when you and she don't get along?

If it doesn't feel right to settle or compromise, don't. And seek support (see below).

Scenario 4: You want 2 opposite things

I'm not going to lie. If you are set for a wedding in a castle in the South of France with 200+ guests and your spouse can only dream of an intimate elopement with only you, the dog and an officiant in the desert of Kalahari, you're up for a good challenge. But absolutely not an impossible one.

The goal is always to support each other's vision and wishes. The question to ask each other is: "How can I help you bring your dream wedding to life?" We live in a world of dichotomy. It's "either...or..." and you want to switch to unity: "both...and...".

BLISS Coaching Question: Time to get creative! Answer the question: "How can you both have what you want?"

For the last 2 scenarios, I'd say 3 important things:
1. Don't make compromises, unless you're absolutely certain that you will not regret them later.
2. Don't worry. It's not uncommon or unsurmountable. Take a few deep breaths and don't see it as a negative sign. Remember that opposite attracts.
3. Seek help from someone neutral and objective .

And if you've enjoyed this book so far, I've got you! Feel free to reach out to me at book@blissbycaroline.com, or use the QR code at the end of the book to book a call and tell me more about your challenges. I'll be happy to assist you and share resources to help you navigate your unique situation.

CHAPTER 8

Sharing Your Vision

Once you've aligned the vision with your spouse, the last step will be to share it with those involved with your wedding planning. It is crucial for 3 reasons:

1. It will bring everyone on board to bring to life the vision you hold
2. You will be able to have a reality check on what's actually possible
3. It's also the opportunity to ensure your vision is crisp and clear for other people

Have you ever seen the Minions? These adorably annoying little yellow creatures who speak their own language that no one understands but themselves? Well, sometimes we are so into our own bubble that we don't realize that we either don't make sense for people outside of our bubble, or that we are not able to articulate our vision in a way that others can grasp it fully.

Or do you know Olaf, the snowman in the Disney movie Frozen, who dreams about Summer all the time but doesn't realize that a snowman in summer is essentially a death sentence?

Sharing your vision to your friends, family, and vendors will give you this last check and opportunity to fine tune your plan. Like Olaf, you want others to let you know when your ideas are not going to turn out so well for you in the end.

And that's why building a dream team becomes instrumental. In the next section, I want to help you make intentional decisions about the people you will surround yourself with for your wedding planning journey. Because guess what? A great team will ease your experience, lower your stress, bring your vision to life and make this entire journey so much more enjoyable. And isn't that exactly what you want?

SECTION 3
Enjoyment Enhancers

CHAPTER 9

Why Building A Dream Team Is Crucial

Have you ever heard the saying "You're the average of the 5 people you spend the most time with?"

Kellogg Insight ran a study and discovered that sitting within a 25-foot radius of a high performer increases your work performance by 15%, while sitting within the same distance of a poor performer can decrease your performance by up to 30%. It's called the spillover effect.

> *"Once a toxic person shows up next to you, your risk of becoming toxic yourself has gone up."*
> *- Dylan Minor*

It is true at work and in any other life setting, and your wedding planning is no exception. If there is one thing that I'd like you to take away from this book it's this: how you surround yourself will determine the quality of your existence. If there is nothing else you do as you prepare your wedding, please do this: build a team that will elevate your experience, support you and make it possible for you to show up as the very best version of yourself.

I can't reinforce this enough. No matter how strong you are or think you are, if a new neighbor shows up on your street with loud distasteful music that they play every evening from the sidewalk, it will inevitably affect the tranquility of your own home (and if this sounds like a real experience, you're absolutely right. It is!)

Another important point: you can have the best team at home, if you have a toxic coworker it will absolutely affect not just work but all other areas of your life. While I will only cover specifically how to navigate challenging relationships in the context of your wedding planning, know that the tools I'll be sharing in later chapters will help you for any relationship. You're welcome ;).

Whether we are talking about the vendors you select, the family members you involve, or your friends helping and supporting you on the way, every single person you bring on your team must be intentionally chosen.

In the next chapters we'll explore how to assemble the best team of professionals and vendors, and we'll then discuss the sensitive topic of managing family dynamics.

Stress-free Wedding

CHAPTER 10

Selecting Your Dream Team

A wedding is a collaborative effort, and assembling the right team of professionals is crucial to transforming your vision into reality. From capturing your love story to crafting the perfect culinary experience, your vendors play a pivotal role in creating an unforgettable celebration.

Selecting The Right Vendors For You

Imagine being a football coach and now you need to hire each player and team member to win big at the championship. Who would you pick?

You want pros: Avoid settling for Martha, your friend from high school who's a great home cook as your caterer if food is important to you. Or taking Bob, the friend of a friend of your neighbor as your wedding photographer just because his flower shots are amazing if pictures rank high in your list. That's not to say to not give newbies a chance but make sure you pick the pros where you want them most.

You want them to follow your lead: You hold the vision and they will help you bring it to life. They can enhance it but not change the plans or go their own ways. Hence why having a crisp shared and aligned vision with your partner is crucial as you meet prospective vendors.

You want to enjoy their company: You're about to spend a lot of time with your wedding team, many back and forth communications, oh so many emails and texts. Select vendors you trust and connect with on a personal level.

You Get What You Give

You get to choose how you want the relationship to go. You can treat the experts you are bringing on board as vendors, but I believe you will have a much better experience if you forge deeper relationships with them.

My husband has shot 300+ weddings as I write these lines. You think your celebration is going to be unique? Of course it will. But when he tells his clients their timeline is unrealistic, you get to choose to boss him around (and realize on the day that he was right - I have yet to watch the scene unfold any differently in over a decade) or you can lean into his experience, trust him and leverage his perspective on how to update the timeline to a realistic place and so you have the best possible shots.

Same is true for all your vendors. It's not their first rodeo (oh well wedding…) ;).

Most (if not all) of the dream team members you select will witness the most vulnerable and difficult moments of your wedding planning and your wedding day. They will hear and see the good, the bad, and the ugly. My point for you here is to choose the people you feel comfortable around, the ones who make you feel calm, and in good hands. You want professionals who take the time to understand you and your unique love story. You want people who care.

How To Select Your Dream Team

Here is what I highly recommend you do as you embark on your selection journey:

1. **Ask for Recommendations:** Seek recommendations from friends, family, and other couples who have recently married. This can be a huge time saver! You get to leverage the work that others have done before you, all while being able to get their perspective and experience. Definitely start there!

2. **Do Your Research:** Start early and research the vendors who caught your eye. Look for reviews, recommendations, and online portfolios. Make sure that what you read and see matches your vision as well as the mood and energy you want for your wedding day.

3. **Set a Budget:** Determine your wedding budget and allocate funds for each vendor category. Your prioritization exercise will become very helpful here.

4. Meet: Schedule consultations with potential vendors to assess their personality, professionalism, and compatibility with your vision.

5. Read Contracts Carefully: Avoid any surprises. Before signing any contracts, carefully review the terms and conditions, including pricing, cancellation policies, and payment schedules.

6. Ask Questions: Don't hesitate to ask vendors questions about their experience, availability, and services, or anything that is important to you.

7. Trust Your Gut: If you feel uncomfortable or unsure about a vendor, trust your intuition and get to the next one on the list.

Selecting your dream team is a two-way street. It's not about them choosing you or vice versa. It's like selecting a spouse. For the marriage to be successful you want both parties to be a "Hell Yes!"

SECTION 4
Your Biggest Stressors

CHAPTER 11

Yes, It's Finally Time To Talk About Your In-Laws (And Other Challenging Family Dynamics)

Selecting vendors should feel like a piece of cake compared to family dynamics. You might think that you have the best of relationships with your family and in-laws, and yet, a wedding has a way of bringing up some of the most hidden tensions to the surface.

Weddings are a celebration of love, but they can also be a delicate balancing act, particularly when family is involved. Navigating differing opinions, expectations, and personalities requires tact, self-control, empathy, and effective communication.

It's draining, time-consuming, overwhelming, and frustrating. I get it!

If your mother-in-law drives you up the wall, you're not alone. Many couples face challenges with parents (and in-laws) when planning their wedding.

Most Common Parents Challenges

- **Over-involvement:** From dress drama to guest list control, your parents have got an opinion on everything. You're open to suggestions but it sounds more like criticism at times.
- **Financial Concerns:** Because they pitch in financially they think it gives them a right of say and that's not to your liking.
- **Historical Tension:** Let's be straight here: you never really clicked with your in-laws (or you have unresolved challenges with your own parents) and the wedding planning makes it quite visible for everyone to see.

Your Parents & In-Laws Care

I personally assume that everyone has good intentions and sometimes poor ways of showing them. You know your own people, so I'll let you be the judge of their character. But I always like to remind my clients that most people don't wake up in the morning asking themselves "how can I ruin the day of my kid's future spouse today?"

If you think they do, please make sure to stay as far as you can from them for your own safety and sanity.

Hopefully you don't think it's the case and you are dealing with parents who care (a little bit too much), with poor emotional intelligence, suboptimal communication skills, and a very low understanding of human psychology. I'm essentially being polite here, hope you appreciate my demonstration of keeping my cool ;).

Regardless of their intentions, they make planning your wedding soul-sucking at times and that's what I'm here to help you with.

Your Options

If your relationship with your parents or in-laws isn't amazing, you have a choice to make:

Option 1: You suck it up! I won't judge you if you choose that route because I know how the alternative can feel. If you choose to bite your tongue and do your best to keep your cool though, I want to inform you of a risk. It's very likely that by giving in you are setting a precedent for how they will treat you now and in the future. That said, choosing this route now doesn't mean you can't make a different decision in the future. But I'd argue that now is a very good time to shape the relationship for good. So why not?

OR

Option 2: You step into your brave side and you take this as an opportunity to change the dynamic of the relationship you have with them for good. You address the behavior, the criticism, the tension in an emotionally detached but firm way.

Preparing For Your Options

If you choose the "suck it up" route, what you will need is a solid strategy to cope with the situation. And if you choose to set the record straight now, you will need a good scoop of courage and serenity.

Either way, and in my opinion, the best way to proceed is to develop a deep sense of self-worth and self-confidence, so that when anyone shows up in your space with a vibe that's not grooving with you, you are profoundly fine. Not faking it!

Self-Love

First, let me debunk a myth. It may not be what you think consciously but there is a big chance that part of you thinks this way unconsciously: Loving yourself is NOT selfish. Loving yourself is NOT being full of yourself. Loving yourself is NOT about loving you more than you love others.

Self-love means finding peace within ourselves, cultivating a warm and nurturing attitude toward what we experience inside. It means having empathy and unconditional positive regard for ourselves: what we think, what we feel, who we are…

We find it easy and natural to be gentle and kind with others, and we let the little voice inside, our inner critic, take over to the point of forgetting to have the same kindness for ourselves.

Tonya Leigh, the master coach and founder of the School of Self-Image once offered this distinction that I love. I'm paraphrasing what she said here but essentially: "If your child or someone you love deeply came to you on a low day saying: "I feel like shit!" or "I'm a loser." would you respond: "Oh yeah baby you don't just feel like shit, you look like shit today!" or "Absolutely true dear, you are a loser."? Probably not!'

The truth is even if you think they look like shit or are a loser in the context of the conversation (because we are human and have a tendency to be critical) we would try to cheer them up, see the bright side and comfort them.

Well, self-love is doing this to yourself. It's accepting that we may feel low but not adding more criticism and finding ways to cheer ourselves up.

Step-by-step guide to loving oneself

Loving yourself is the work of a lifetime because we change, we grow, we age, and at every season of our lives we have a new version of ourselves to discover and nurture. The reward is the most extraordinary of all, because it has a ripple effect on everything in our life: career, relationships, body, finances… and more.

Here is a step-by-step guide to help you cultivate self-love, along with some tools you can use right away.

1. Be Kind to Yourself: Treat yourself with the same care as a friend.
- Forgive your mistakes
- Accept your flaws

2. Take Care of You:
- Eat well, sleep enough, and move your body (remember the non-negotiable RED in Chapter 4?)
- Relax and unwind
- Create a comfy space

3. Think Good Thoughts:
- Focus on your strengths
- Replace negative thoughts with positive ones
- Imagine yourself happy and successful

4. Set Limits:
- Know what you can handle
- Say no when you need to
- Prioritize your needs

5. Connect and Share:
- Spend time with supportive people
- Help others to feel good
- Find a group with similar interests
- Do things you enjoy

Remember: Progress takes time. Be patient with yourself, celebrate small victories, and don't be afraid to seek support from a professional if needed.

Two Tools for Self-Love

Tool #1 - Mirror Tool: Take lipstick or a marker and write "I love myself" on every mirror of your home. Every time you see your reflection, say it out loud "I love myself".

Tool #2 - Your own haka: Create a daily routine where you can repeat a series of statements meant to nurture self-love, such as "I am beautiful. I am smart. I love myself."

A haka is a traditional Māori dance from New Zealand. It's a powerful and energetic performance that uses rhythmic movements, chanting, and facial expressions to convey emotions like strength, unity, and challenge. Think of it as a way to show pride, honor, or even a warning to others.

Haka are often performed in groups, and they can be used for various occasions, like welcoming guests, celebrating achievements, or before a competition. The most famous haka is probably the one performed by the New Zealand All Blacks rugby team before their matches.

To cultivate self-love in our family, JL and I have created a bedtime ritual with Louise. Before we turn off the lights we repeat this short choreography where we all say out loud: "I am smart. I am strong. I am funny. I am beautiful. I had an amazing day. I am healthy. I love me. I love my family."

The mirror tool and the haka may seem silly or trivial but there's a reason why they work. If you remember our chapters about beliefs, a belief is a thought that you repeat to yourself so much that it becomes, well, a belief. If you repeat kind things to yourself about yourself you create new beliefs. You can say it in your head, but if you want faster and more powerful results, say it out loud and feel it in your heart. You want to elicit a positive emotion. That's why we have added choreography to our bedtime routine. You can add music too. Whatever helps!

It All Comes Down To Habits

Learning to love yourself comes down to creating new habits, which will generate new beliefs about yourself. Some of these new thoughts of kindness and compassion will help you show up as a different person and take radically new actions.

Are you thinking: *"When is she finally going to tell me what to do with my mother-in-law?!"*

We're getting there! I promise.

Why Self-Love Is The Solution To All Your Relationship Problems

Imagine walking into a large ballroom (think Le Grand Palais in Paris or the Egypt aisle of the Metropolitan Museum of Art in New York), a majestic, grandiose space filled with an elegant party. All the guests are wearing their fanciest outfits, everyone is at their best. People mingle, there is chatter and light music in the background.

You are about to enter this space alone and you know no one. All of it is unfamiliar to you.

There are 2 versions of that entrance.

The first one is you, not loving yourself fully. You have some self-image challenges (your nose, your legs, your shape…). As you watch the space, all sorts of insecurities creep in: you could have done a better job with your hair. You don't feel like you belong there. Everyone looks so stunning and impeccable. Who are you to walk in that room?

When that version of you walks in, here's what's going to happen: no matter how confident you will try to appear, your insecurities will rise. You may speak quickly because of your stress level being high. You may miss a step on the staircase, you will rush to the buffet and stick there like a koala hugging a tree all evening.

The second version of you about to make an entrance has their head up high and feels unapologetically confident. You feel awesome regardless of what others might think or say. This version of you doesn't need anything or anyone. They want things and they simply go get them. As you step in the door you walk confidently like you own the place. Of course you feel stress but you use it to fuel your actions, not to limit them.

Can you see how differently the room would interact with each version of you? As I think about the first version, I picture someone trying to make themselves as small and invisible as possible. While the second one takes space. I wouldn't mess with the latter version of you entering that party.

And that is exactly what you want with your in-laws, and frankly anyone you interact with.

Now notice that a confident version of you walking into the party doesn't harm anyone. You don't bulldoze or criticize others to feel grand. You are simply grand.

I have recorded a short video about this that you can check out using the QR code on the last page of this book.

How To Deal Practically With Challenging Family Dynamics

As we largely discussed, step 1 is to gradually learn to cultivate self-love, and step 2 is to remind yourself that whatever they do to you probably comes from a good place.

But now it is time to address the problems head-on!

As a general rule, don't fight power with power or you'll escalate it to a war. If your father makes a snarky comment about your partner, getting defensive or making a snarky comment in return will only make things worse. And we all want peace, ease and calm.

You Get...

I live by 4 sayings that I go back to every time it seems like I can't get what I want.

Ready?
- You get what you give.
- You get what you expect.
- You get what you tolerate.
- You get what you ask for.

And that is the framework we'll use to help you navigate any challenging dynamics with family, friends, vendors (and even colleagues or strangers).

What Do You Want To Get?

Your shared vision comes in very handy here again. Take a moment, alone or with your partner, and think about how you would like each member of your family and friends to support the execution of your vision.

BLISS Coaching Question: Has Aunt May always been your go-to for anything flower-related? Is your best friend amazing at everything but helping you with style? Do you dread spending time with your parents? Be honest and ask yourself, if you could decide whatever you please without fear of the consequences, who would you turn to for help, and who would you least involve?

"Great Caroline! But I can't tell my parents to stay put while I involve my Aunt! Especially as they are funding a large portion of my wedding?!"

I hear you! Again you can choose between actually standing your ground and telling your parents the truth ("I'd love the money and limited involvement from you guys." And yes that may feel like a rough chat but dare I say a necessary one?) or you can give them a job that won't take too much of your bandwidth or that is lower in your priority list but that you know they would be good at!

Has mom always been good with entertaining guests or kids? Well, she's hired!

Regardless of how amazing or challenging your family relationship is, remember to think about it with as much compassion and love as you can.

"Be kind, for everyone you meet is fighting a hard battle"
- Plato

You Get What You Give - Let's Give

You want your family to treat you with respect and kindness (and they currently aren't). Lead by example and don't default into attack or defense mode.

Your sister-in-law makes an awful comment about your lack of style in public? Don't get back at her. Take her aside and address the comment in private (the respect and kindness she didn't give you). You can ask her firmly but kindly that she keeps any criticism about you to herself or that she brings her opinion about you to you first.

You Get What You Expect - Let's Expect

If you think your parents will never support your decision to marry your partner and will never give them a chance, you're setting yourself up for failure. But if you expect with deep confidence that with more time they will come around and you are willing to give them the space they need to know and love your future spouse, well it will most likely happen. Your entire demeanor will shift and they will be most likely to meet your expectations even without talking about it. They will sense it's a non-negotiable for you.

You Get What You Tolerate - Let's Tolerate

If your father-in-law is treating you like you will never belong in their family and you let his show go on, you will set a precedent where his baseline will be to treat you poorly. You are allowed to stand up for yourself. Again with as much compassion and love you are capable of and always with respect. "I understand we still need to get to know each other more but I want to reiterate how much I'm looking forward to it."

You Get What You Ask For - Let's Ask

You may think that what you want is obvious but it's not. Some people are afraid to ask for more help and rage when no one spontaneously offers to support, while some don't want help and love to do it alone and hate when people proactively help thinking it's nice of them.

Just ask. What would you like to receive from others? Say it explicitly. It's simple and straightforward and will save you so much time and energy.

With these tools a lot of problems will be avoided. Conflicts however are unavoidable. Next, let's talk about 2 major conflicts couples face when planning their wedding: conflicts with people, and conflict about money.

CHAPTER 12

Navigating Conflicts

First of all let's remind ourselves that conflict is bound to happen and that it can be healthy and managed with ease and calm. So let's make room for it. Disagreements and arguments are a sign that all parties are passionate and involved. The goal is not to win at the expense of others, it's to welcome the discussion with an open-mind and genuine curiosity.

That said we all would rather minimize conflict. Here are some of the fundamentals to apply today to ensure the smoothest journey on your wedding planning path.

Setting Boundaries and Communicating Needs

Establishing clear boundaries is essential for maintaining harmony with your loved ones during the wedding planning process.
- **Open Dialogue:** Have honest conversations about your expectations and limitations
- **Define Roles:** Clearly outline the roles and responsibilities of everyone involved in the planning
- **Set Limits:** Establish boundaries regarding involvement in decision-making to avoid conflict

Compromise and Collaboration

Weddings often involve merging two families and two sets of friends, which can lead to differing opinions on various aspects of the celebration.
- **Active Listening:** Encourage open communication and actively listen to your families' perspectives

- **Prioritize Your Relationship:** Remember that your relationship with your partner is the foundation of your wedding. Make room for it.

Managing Expectations

Unrealistic expectations can lead to disappointment and conflict.
- **Communicate Clearly:** Clearly communicate your budget, guest list, and wedding vision to your families and close friends
- **Set Realistic Expectations:** Help your families understand the complexities of wedding planning
- **Seek Support:** Lean on your partner for support and encouragement when dealing with family-related challenges

By approaching personal dynamics with empathy, open communication, and a willingness to compromise, you can create a harmonious and enjoyable wedding planning experience.

The Talk

If you've tried all the "soft" approaches and it's not working, maybe it's time to actually have a talk with whomever is making your wedding planning journey challenging.

If you get there, I'd love to share with you a great tool to frame your conversation in a way that maximizes your chance of getting what you want without damaging the relationship.

Nonviolent Communication

Nonviolent Communication (NVC) is a method of communication, developed by Marshall Rosenberg that is focused on building understanding and connection. It helps people share their feelings and needs openly, without blame or judgment. The goal isn't to eliminate disagreements but to create a space where everyone feels heard and valued.

Let me walk you through how it works with an example.

Imagine that your stepmother was being dismissive, and making the wedding planning process very difficult for you to enjoy. She felt entitled to the planning, as her and your father were contributing a large part to your wedding. While grateful for their contribution, you feel like she is treating your wedding like her day, and not giving you or your partner any say. She made a rough criticism about your inability to be on time with anything in front of your wedding planner and caterer and this felt like the cherry on the cake for you. That said, you don't want to ruin your relationship with her over wedding planning...

NVC offers a great way to stand your ground in a non-emotional way and yet to address the problem.

Here's how it works:
1- State the problem without emotions:
"Hi Jane, I'd love to talk to you about the wedding planning. Do you have 5 minutes for me right now? Awesome!

Here's what I observe:

You are making a large contribution to our wedding in the planning process and are making many decisions without taking our perspective into account, like the seating chart.

You are making comments about your belief that I have a poor sense of timing publicly.

And that doesn't contribute to my well-being or my enjoyment of preparing for my wedding."

2- State how it makes you feel

"I feel dismissed and criticized…"

Remember that what you feel is INDISPUTABLE. They are YOUR feelings period.

3- Share your needs firmly

"…because what I need is to love planning my wedding. I need it to look like me and Ellis. And I want to remember this wedding planning journey as a moment that got us all happy and closer together."

4- Make a request

"Would you be willing to consider a different way of planning this wedding together?"

You can elaborate with something like "If you are open to it we can meet on Sunday, you, me, dad and Ellis and discuss how to make this enjoyable for everyone. What do you say?"

Note: I highly advise that you write your script down and rehearse it. This approach works powerfully if you stay on script and don't wing it. If you go with the flow you may insert judgment or blame and it may not end as well, or as planned.

As you go with your script don't let her interrupt you.

If she does, pause, let her finish (and don't pay attention to anything she says) and respond "I'd like to finish what I have to say without being interrupted. Would you think that's possible? Great!.. So I was saying…" and you return to your script.

From there she has 2 options:

1- Get defensive, and go on with all the reasons why she's right, or why your feelings are stupid, or how it's not her intention but if she wasn't there nothing would get done because the vendors you chose are this and that…

If that's the route she chooses, again disregard the content of what she's saying and answer: "So are you saying that you are not willing to operate differently at all? And both me and Ellis have no other option than to follow your lead for our wedding. Is that what you are saying?" (make sure to keep a neutral voice and tone).

OR

2- She's wise and accepts your proposition. If so, simply say "I'm so grateful for you. Thank you so much. It means a lot to me."

From that point on ALWAYS return to the NVC framework to deal with her behavior. Like anything, people need repetition and time to understand things that are new to them. Eventually she will stop because she will fully integrate the fact that you never let this type of behavior fly.

BLISS Coaching Question: Is there a situation that you would like to address? If so, use the Nonviolent Communication framework and write down your script using the 4 steps above. Once you're done writing it, rehearse with someone neutral to the issue and ask if it is clear and factual (as in non judgmental).

Purple Hair

There might be times where you are ready to address criticism on the spot. And I would love to share with you my Purple Hair framework.

Imagine you're having a date with your bestie. You love them, they've been part of your life for years. You two know so much about each other and you are always blunt and honest. You're having a great lunch with them. You go to the bathroom. As you come back, your friend looks embarrassed and tells you that it's best to leave the restaurant right away.

You're confused. You haven't had dessert yet? What happened while you were away that changed the plan so drastically? So you ask "What's going on?"

"I don't know how to say this without hurting your feelings. But why? Why did you do that?" they're pointing at your hair and now you're even more lost in translation.

"Why did I do what?" you ask.

"Your hair! Why did you color it purple? You look both stupid and ugly…" they say.

Now you're full blown panicked and your mind is racing. Last time you checked (which was just a minute or so ago in the bathroom) your hair was perfectly normal and definitely not purple. Plus, you would remember coloring your hair purple. Also, why say this to you now? It's not like you look any different than before going to the bathroom…

For a sanity check, you grab your phone and turn it to selfie mode to check your hair again and it is definitely not purple.

Now you realize your friend is either having a seizure or something that requires a 911 call.

"Are you okay?" you ask. "Do you feel lightheaded or weird or something?" And you start to worry about them.

See in this example, you would not take the criticism at face value. Yes, sure you will most likely check that your hair didn't magically change color but you would quickly turn your attention away from their comment, away from you and toward them. Because you are so confident about your hair color that the criticism doesn't register for you.

That's how I'm inviting you to navigate a snarky comment or criticism moving forward. Because often the comment has NOTHING TO DO WITH YOU. Yes I wrote this in caps because you need to read this.

Let's return to the stepmother situation we mentioned earlier. As she makes a criticism insinuating that you're always late to everything you can tackle this with my

Purple Hair framework and leveraging some of the concepts we covered so far.

1- Love yourself so much you have unshakeable self-confidence
2- Treat her with the respect, dignity and compassion you want to receive (and that she haven't given you)
3- Purple Hair her

It can go like this:
1- Take a deep breath and repeat in your head your haka or your mirror statement (from Chapter 11)
2- Take her aside and ask to chat privately "Hey Jane, can I talk to you privately right now?"
3- Ask with genuine concern "Are you feeling alright? The comment you just made about me being late to everything sounded harsh and not something I would expect from you, especially in public. Is there anything I should be worried about?"

Most people who make public criticism don't expect you to address it right away and definitely don't think you would come with calm, and detachment. Try it and watch how things can shift magically.

If your stepmother was getting defensive then you can NVC her. But once you accept that her comment has TRULY NOTHING TO DO WITH YOU (yes, I did it all in caps again!) it gets easier to talk in a factual way and not an emotional way.

If after all these tools you still feel like your challenges are unaddressed, send me an email (at book@blissbycaroline.com) and tell me more. I'll gladly support you.

Next we're going to talk about another elephant in the room: $$$

CHAPTER 13

Let's Talk About Money

Creating a realistic and achievable wedding budget is essential for stress-free planning. By establishing financial parameters, you can make informed decisions and avoid overspending. And for that, any good planner or a generative AI tool will help you with the step-by-step plan to create a realistic budget.

What I want to help you with is to assess the quality of your relationship with money and ensure you work on healing any wound, so that budget is not another source of unnecessary tension. Our ability to healthily manage our finances (or not) is only amplified when planning a wedding.

Spend What You Have

Growing up in Europe, the way we approach money is very different from how it's done in the United States. In France, you can't spend money you don't already have in the bank other than a formal loan or mortgage. Credit card debt isn't exactly a thing. The idea of swiping a credit card to book your venue without having funds to cover it is synonymous with massive long-term financial problems. Fairly quickly, within a month or so, all your bank accounts will get locked and it will be very hard to access it or open a new bank account for a long time. So we grow up learning to live within our means.

When JL and I got married one thing we were constantly debating was: do we spend so much money on a party (aka a wedding) or on a down-payment for a house? And we thought that the house felt more aligned to both of us. Hence why we never ended up throwing a wedding celebration since our civil wedding 10 years ago. Do we regret the decision? Absolutely not! Even if having a fun party with our close friends and family is something we missed. It was a personal choice. And you get to make yours.

If you hadn't realized it yet, I'm big on following my intuition, my guts if you will. Free yourself from what's conventional and acceptable, and do what YOU want.

That said, I'd highly recommend that for your wedding you stay within your means. Not starting your marriage on debt is a healthy standard to set and will significantly reduce your stress now and after your wedding day.

Choose Your Financial Priorities

Society has created a narrative around money that's not the healthiest and it may be impacting your relationship to your finances. We tie our self-worth to our possessions which gives us access to a status in society, all of which is directly tied to money we have, money we owe, and money we spend.

I love Ramit Sethi's saying " Choose your rich". The Netflix host of "I Will Teach You To Get Rich" is a millionaire who drives an old, cheap Honda but also wears expensive Burberry sweaters. He shares that he loves sweaters and pays attention to his outfit but he only wants a car to drive him from point A to point B.

BLISS Coaching Question: My invitation to you as you plan your wedding is to get super clear on selecting where you would splurge on a 3-step podium. Ask yourself, if you could only spend money on 3 things for your wedding, what would they be? Do it alone and then share it with your spouse to discuss and align on your combined priorities.

Talk About Money

My husband JL and I have a "CFO (Chief Financial Officer) meeting" twice a month for 10 minutes.
1. The first meeting is the week before the first week of the month,
2. And the second meeting is the week before the 15th of the month.

Both being aligned to when most of our bills hit.

I prepare our budget tracker and we review our expenses and upcoming bills along with our income to see how we are trending. It's a formal meeting and I know it may sound dry but here are the reasons why I advise you to put in place such a practice (whether or not you share a joint account or keep your accounts separate):

- **Constant (re)alignment:** Heraclitus said "the only constant in life is change". Taking time frequently to ensure that you are both still aligned or to adjust to the changes in your financial situation will eliminate potential misunderstanding and unnecessary stress.
- **Transparency:** When you don't talk about your finances frequently it is easy to make assumptions or to lose track with reality. Meeting at least once a month ensures that you both have a crisp view on your finances.
- **Accountability:** When you know that you are meeting at a fixed cadence with your partner, you make yourself accountable to decisions, like who pays what, or how much you plan on saving. It therefore increases your chances of staying on track with your money goals.
- **Support:** If any of you face some difficulties, these meetings will allow the other one to step in. It's also an opportunity to tap into each of your strengths as it relates to money. If one of you is good at saving and the other one at spending, you get to

leverage each other's strengths to achieve your common goals.

Marriage is about going from "me" to "we" in all areas of life, including your finances, regardless of how enjoyable or sexy this topic is for you.

And, as always, feel free to reach out if you'd like to get help with other money-related challenges at book@blissbycaroline.com.

SECTION 5
Your Wedding Day

SECTION 5
Your Wedding Day

CHAPTER 14

Enjoying Your Blissful Day

You've made it! The big day has finally arrived. You've poured your heart into planning your wedding. Hopefully everything goes smoothly. But possibly something(s) may not go as you wished. In this chapter, I want to help you shift your mindset from preparation mode to celebration mode.

Your Only Strategy

My best piece of advice for you on your wedding day is to enjoy it. Be fully present, because the day is going to be gone in a flash. Soon, all you'll have left of it are memories, pictures, videos, your outfit and your rings (and maybe a good headache the next morning).

I met a wedding photographer who told me this story and it stuck with me since. She was shooting a wedding while her spouse was undergoing surgery. Her husband was diagnosed with cancer at an advanced stage. She had booked her clients a year in advance - before the diagnosis was made. She and her husband knew that the alternative was her sitting in a waiting room for hours and that it wouldn't change the outcome of the surgery. So she decided to honor the commitment to her clients.

At the wedding, the bride threw a massive fit when the ribbon of her bridal bouquet wasn't the exact shade of yellow she expected. She made it a huge deal and was very upset. The pictures of a portion of the day were ruined by her facial expression, and the getting ready unfolded in a tense atmosphere. No one had fun for a moment. All while this photographer checked her phone waiting to hear the life prognosis of her husband. To her the scene was surreal. It's not like the flowers were a completely different color (and even so). The photographer's husband's life was on the line and she kept her composure and commitment to her clients, while the bride couldn't accept a non-life threatening mishap.

I'm not sharing this story to judge the bride, but rather to remind you to keep a proportionate reaction to the potential challenges that may arise. There are worse things that can happen than a delay or a miss on a wedding day.

I remember my husband texting me one day as he was shooting a wedding. "The ceremony is in 20 minutes and my clients don't like the venue anymore. So we are currently all on hold until the couple finds a new venue." Okay, a pretty rare, yet stressful situation. But if you choose to embrace the day with all its imperfections, you may end up having the most memorable and fun wedding day ever.

My point being: enjoy the moment, be present, accept the things that are out of your control and trust that everything will unfold perfectly if you approach it with detachment and calm.

Stress-free Wedding

**BONUS
CHAPTER 15**

You Are The Star Of Your Day

The most distinctive aspect of your wedding day (unless you are a celebrity, in which case you probably don't need this bonus) is that you are going to be the center of attention all day long. And for some of my clients this alone is an anticipated source of anxiety and stress.

So here are a few tips to feel more comfortable in front of the camera.

For this chapter I have partnered with my love & life partner, my amazing husband, and talented photographer, Jean-Laurent Gaudy (JL).

The fun thing about writing this chapter together is:
1. A photographer is rarely comfortable in front of the camera, and JL is no exception to that rule.
2. As a professional photographer he has developed a clear sense of how to make couples more at ease during shoots.

So you will get both his professional tips and my experience from our own couple's photoshoots.

The Voice In Your Head

Self-image issues are mental constructs. We are mostly fine being ourselves until a camera enters the room, and all of a sudden the same moment feels more complicated. That's because we have narratives playing in our subconscious minds about ourselves and our bodies. And the stories it's telling aren't flattering. The problem is not so much the voice in our head as it is the fact that we haven't learned to override it with empowering thoughts.

Naturally, my first tip to you is to get to the root cause of your self-image challenges and decide how you want to feel about yourself. And in case you have any doubt about how to feel, the word is "beautiful" ;).

In my teens, one day we were looking at family pictures with my mom. There was a picture of me wearing shorts and it seemed like my knees were disproportionately big compared to my skinny legs. It made us all laugh. My mom pulled out a sticky note and drew two lines (for my legs) and in the middle two big half circles on each side (my knees). We all laughed wholeheartedly. It became a go-to joke to lighten up the mood for years to come.

I didn't realize it then but this joke left a deep story in my head: my knees look weird. Throughout high-school, college, and my early adult life, I wore pants every day of the week. And when I had my legs bare (at the pool in a swimsuit) I was so self conscious and uncomfortable.

When I started dating JL, he asked why I wasn't wearing skirts or dresses more often - it clicked. This family joke had shaped my self-image. His love, support, and sense of style gave me the confidence to rewrite this story in my head and while it's still less natural for me to show my legs, I don't think about my knees when I wear above-the-knee clothes.

> **BLISS Coaching Question:** What stories are you listening to in your head about your body? Which story is not helpful or empowering? How can you rewrite these stories to serve you and make you feel good about yourself?

Choose Wisely

Selecting a photographer that you vibe with is the most important tip if you struggle with your self-image. A great photographer will know how to best help you ahead of the wedding day and as they are shooting to make you feel more at ease. They will also know how to be there to capture the day without you feeling their omnipresence.

Slow Down & Be Authentic

"A couple with both partners feeling anxious in front of the camera is really challenging for a photographer, but not uncommon. What works best when I face such situations is to slow them down and encourage them to be authentic."
- Jean-Laurent Gaudy

- **Don't force a pose that doesn't feel right**: In my experience when it feels weird, it typically looks weird in the pictures.
- **Be yourself:** From the clothes you pick to the places you go, to what you do during a shoot, choose to be your true, authentic self. Don't try to be someone else or copy something you saw that looked cool. As Oscar Wilde said *"Be yourself; everyone else is already taken."*
- **Support your partner:** If your partner is struggling more than you in front of the camera, take charge. You know how to make them laugh, relax, and forget that a photographer is here, even for a split second.

This last tip is what I've been doing when JL and I are being photographed. While it is often awkward at first I focus on the outcome: the pictures we will get to look at for years. I want to remember the moment as a parenthesis from our busy lives, watch our pictures and see us as we were then. So I engage in a conversation with him, I whisper silly jokes, we get coffee (his favorite thing), I ask him to help me with my hair, anything that will get his attention away from the camera. And let me tell you, the result is magical.

Forget It

"Pictures are some of the very few tangibles you will keep from your wedding day. Forget the camera is here and enjoy this moment with your loved ones."
- Jean-Laurent Gaudy

Direct your focus on your partner, your family and your friends. Take in the love and the fun from that extraordinary instant and trust that the pictures will perfectly reflect the beautiful essence of what you and your spouse have carefully created.

SECTION 6
Your Journey Beyond Your Wedding Day

SECTION 6
Your Journey Beyond Your Wedding Day

CHAPTER 16

It Only Takes You

I became a mother a few months before the pandemic. I knew intellectually how much my life was going to be different but experiencing it is a whole other level. I returned to work from maternity leave a few short weeks before the lockdown and I felt crushed. I was leaving our home before our daughter woke up and came back just in time to put her to bed, 5 days a week.

When we were sent home indefinitely, in March 2020, I rejoiced. I could work and see my baby. The pandemic allowed me to witness all of my kid's firsts while delivering outstanding work performance. I felt like all my career challenges were gone with the proven test of remote work. That was until we were mandated to return to the office early January 2021. It made no logical sense and it disrupted again, my newly found work-life integration.

I tried so hard to make it work but the truth is I was feeling miserable and at the end of my rope. There's a name for that: it's called burnout.

Eventually I chose to quit my successful career, thinking the job was the problem. Weeks after I left I didn't feel any better. When I met a coach, everything changed. She opened my mind to how I had unconsciously contributed to my pain, and she showed me how to grow to a totally new level in my life and career. She inspired me so much that I became a coach as a result.

But then I had a new problem: I was evolving in a new direction with my life but what if JL and the new "me" didn't click anymore? Was I working on feeling better at the cost of my marriage? I'd be lying if I said that navigating this shift in my life had been easy. But here are 2 lessons I absolutely want to share with you.

Love Each Other So Much That Divorce Will Never Be An Option

I have to give it to JL. From the moment we started dating, there has not been one moment where separating would ever be an option in his mind. If it meant he had to figure out on his own how to revive our relationship or make huge compromises he would have. But separating was always out of the question.

Interestingly enough, his parents separated when in his teens, while I grew up with parents who should have separated but didn't until I was an adult. In any case, his mindset made it so that separating was never an option I could entertain, so I had to come up with other ideas. And I decided to try to make it work with me growing to this new version of myself, while he was not investing in the same type of work at the time.

It Doesn't Take Two To Tango

What I have experienced in our marriage (and I have witnessed similar outcomes with clients) is that once you change, the people around you adjust how they respond to you. I was a lot less stressed out, more accepting and curious, and he started to feel better as a result. Our conflicts reduced in frequency and in intensity, our intimacy grew to levels we didn't think were possible, and our daughter also responded to our new vibe.

The reason why I am sharing this with you is because we tend to think that growing in our relationship or marriage requires both parties to be involved. I'd argue that doing your work alone is one of the most extraordinary investments you can ever make. Witnessing the power of your own transformation onto your surroundings is both magical and mind-blowing. So if you ever feel called to work on yourself to enhance your love relationship, do it.

Anne Hathaway and her husband got tattoos when they got married. It's a W on their wrist. When asked for its meaning she explained "Individually we are Whole. Together we are More." (W backwards is M). And I deeply love this approach. Getting married isn't about agreeing on one path and doing it together. It's about allowing and supporting our spouse to go on their journey, knowing they are doing the same for us. It's about following your unique path while holding hands with your lover.

So go ahead, focus on your goals, and support your future spouse's ones. Don't let them be the reason why you are not making enough progress. Do your work and you will see how quickly they catch up to you. Because that's what marriage is for, lifting each other up in good and bad times. For better or worse…

Stress-free Wedding

Afterword

I want to leave you with an important note. You picked this book for a reason. Most likely because you want support as you navigate the challenges of your wedding planning, or maybe you are a wedding professional and you want to expand your tools to support your clients. Maybe you are getting married, maybe you are already married, or maybe you are single. But I know that you took away tools and lessons that you will get to keep for the rest of your life, way past your love relationships. And that makes me so excited for you.

I have a favor to ask: if you've enjoyed the read, please leave a comment to help others find it.

And I would love to hear from you directly. Send me an email at book@blissbycaroline.com and let me know what helped you the most.

Thank you.

With love,
Caroline

P.S.: If you want to learn more about the work we do at BLISS By Caroline, visit www.blissbycaroline.com

The Author

Caroline Lacaille-Gaudy

Previously working for Tiffany & Co. as a successful Marketing executive, striving to excel at all cost, Caroline burned out and transformed her life to become a calming guide to those who have big dreams.
She used to live in chronic stress, attached to the illusion of being in control yet constantly rushing and feeling depleted and overwhelmed.

After her burnout, she became obsessed with crafting a meaningful life with ease, without compromising what mattered most to her: her relationships, starting with her marriage with JL and their daughter, Louise.

On her quest, she discovered tools and teachings that completely transformed her life and had a positive impact on her family. It worked for her and she started sharing what she practiced with many of her clients. And it worked for them too.

In 2024, she officially co-founded BLISS By Caroline with her husband Jean-Laurent Gaudy (an awarded wedding photographer featured in Harper's Bazaar, The New York Times, Over The Moon, The Knot, and more) and now helps couples and individuals navigate their wedding planning journey with unwavering grace, supporting their emotional and mental state to cultivate bliss and nurture a joyful and stress-free experience.

Website: www.blissbycaroline.com

Photo by Jean-Laurent Gaudy.

Caroline Lacaille-Gaudy

Stress-free Wedding

Acknowledgments

This book wouldn't have been possible without the extraordinary support from dear friends, clients and mentors. I would like to express my deepest gratitude to all and I want to recognize some of you in particular:

Sandy - For your unconditional support from the moment we met. Let's not say how long. We'll feel old ;)

Ann - The most generous person I know. I owe you so much. I'm beyond grateful to have you in my life.

Jen - I'm so glad our work relationship grew to such a beautiful friendship. You are the perfect example of a female leader the world needs more of. Thanks for your eagle eye.

Rime - Your kindness, generosity and openness have been an inspiration even before I called you my friend. I thought about you and some of our chats throughout writing this book. You were with me ;)

Felice - For your cheering, and for our rich conversations. To many more years of growth, love and support.

Charles - You've been a gift, an inspiration and a support that changed my life. I'm eternally grateful.

Alice - This book wouldn't exist without your friendship, your coaching and your inputs. Thank you for your unwavering support.

Ela - For your trust and your bluntness. You're a beautiful soul. I look forward to many more years of growth, friendship and breakthroughs.

Greg - For the depth of both our conversations and our friendship. I look forward to our audio messages and our meetings that I cherish every single time.

Ashley - For your unshakeable joy. You were the surprise I didn't know I needed back then and it's still true to this day. Your friendship and trust means the world to me.

Caroline - I've loved your authenticity and vulnerability in any of our exchanges. Thank you for your support. I look forward to meeting you in person.

Flora - You made publishing a book easy. I appreciate your encouragement and support. Thank you from the bottom of my heart.

I'm grateful for your inputs, edits and most of all for your friendship.

With love,
Caroline

Stress-free Wedding

Access The Bonuses

S can the QR code to access additional resources I have prepared to help you on your wedding planning journey.

Or visit https://www.blissbycaroline.com/book-bonus

Made in the USA
Middletown, DE
05 November 2024